Dear Momma...

written by
Dr. Catherine Murphy

illustrated by
Ira Baykovska

Dear Momma...

ISBN: 978-1-960111-02-9

Library of Congress: 2021911421

Names, characters, and places are products of the author's imagination.
Front cover image, illustrations, and book design by Ira Baykovska.
First printing edition 2021.

Published by Rodney K Press
rodneykpress.com

Visit the author's website @ www.drcatherinemurphy.com

Dear Momma... is dedicated to every mom that has been told that breastfeeding is natural and thus should come naturally. The reality of the breastfeeding journey often differs from what was imagined.

This book comes from a place of compassion and support. Daily, difficult decisions are made by moms for their babies that have no voice. With each step, they learn and grow as caregivers and as strong individuals. The lessons learned from my son opened my eyes to new possibilities in my approach to the health of my family, myself, and patients.

My son struggled to sleep, eat, and manage tummy time. It took countless hours of research and a team of professionals to realize that he had a tongue and lip tie. My son's tongue and lip tie (also known as a restricted tongue, restricted lip, tethered oral tissues, TOTs, ankyloglossia, congenital malformation) contributed to:

- tight muscles
- mouth breathing
- loud breathing
- nursing difficulties
- excessive spit-up
- poor sleep
- difficult swallowing

If you are concerned about your baby having any persistent symptoms, follow your intuition and be persistent in finding appropriate care.

Dear Momma... is also dedicated to my son, Patrick. Thank you Patrick for being patient as I dealt with my own fears and insecurities. Our struggles have led to incredible transformations. As Nana says, *"I love you the whole outside full."*

We thought it would be easy.
It's natural so they say.
But you and I have found out
that there's more than just one way.

Our journey of breastfeeding
may help others if shared,
the way you sought the answers
and how brave you were though scared.

You welcomed me with love
and put me upon your chest.

Your smile and sweet embrace,
I thought we both would rest.

My sleep short and my breath heavy,
I tried and tried to eat.
Although my belly ached for more,
we finally fell asleep.

Someone came to wake us
and recorded all my feedings.
We tried again but couldn't latch,
despite my many pleadings.

You held me upways, sideways
and worry crossed your face.

They told us it may take some time
then left without a trace.

Home, relaxed
with cuddles,
daytime was the
best!

I'd doze and coo, you'd
smile and chuckle,
while bonding upon your
chest.

'Twas nighttime that I struggled.
In my crib alone would cry.
My belly was not full enough
from lack of milk supply.

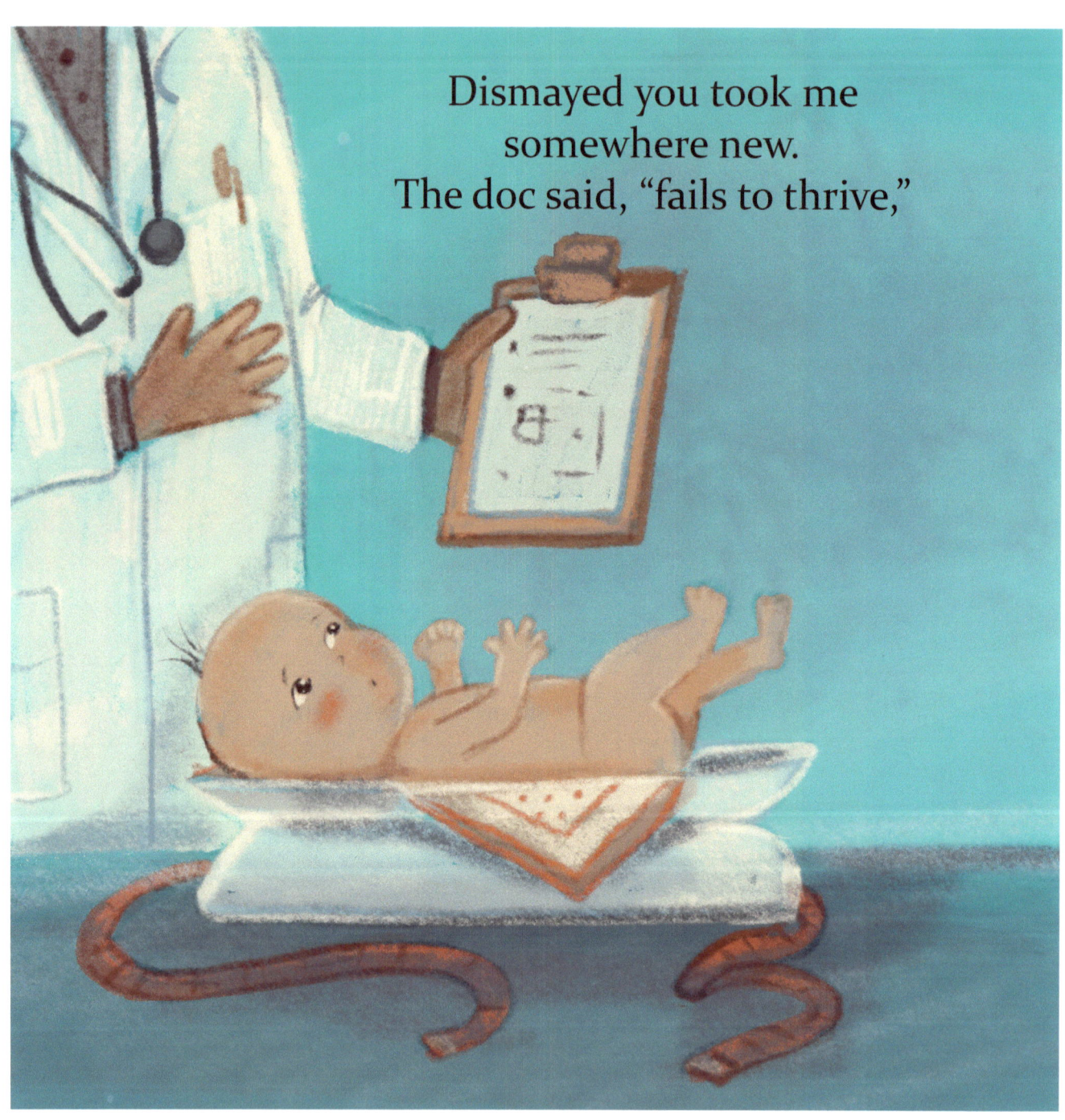

Dismayed you took me
somewhere new.
The doc said, "fails to thrive,"

from bonding to the bottle

shifting focus
to survive.

Rx - formula
Sx - baby not
gaining weight.
No additional
therapies
recommended.

My belly full
but not quite the same.
Momma, you looked
so stressed.

DON'T CRY OVER
SPILLED MILK...

UNLESS IT'S
BREAST MILK

You nursed, then pumped
and bottle-fed
while repeating,
"I'm truly blessed."

Then spit up, hiccups, and tummy time shrieking,
and more advice given, you cried.
The movements were painful and try
as I might, I couldn't express to you why.

Thank you for
not giving up on this,
researching,
and chasing the why.

Wanting more than to hear,
"It's common, don't worry,"
upon scrolling, discovered tongue tie.

New doctors and therapies helped you and me;
things shifted and began to feel right.
Play became fun, no tummy time tears.
Your smile turned hopeful and bright.

Finally...

It all came together; my tongue was released.
You were nervous, I could tell.
Yes, I cried but I was okay.
Once in your arms, all was well.

Momma, please know I thank you.
We are more than goals on charts.

I'm so grateful for your persistence
and I love you with all of my heart.

This journey is like no other.
It is sweet though sometimes tough.

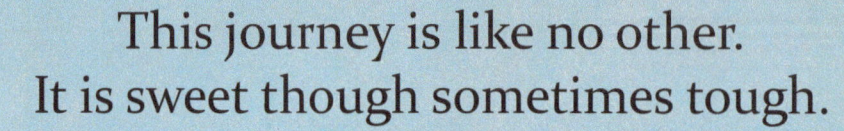

The choices you make for
one with no voice,
Mom, you are more than
enough.

Mom to Mom Wisdom

"Someone once told me motherhood is like trying to stand up on a hammock without spilling your wine. Give yourself grace (and then a little more) and let whatever you do be enough because it is." **Chelsea Pinto**

"I didn't learn to love being a mom until I got rid of my preconceived expectations. Don't sacrifice your 'self' in the pursuit of being the perfect parent." **Tara Erson**

"You were chosen as your child's mama for a reason. You have and are capable of everything they need. You are enough. You will learn and grow together in this beautiful journey." **Christina Irvin**

"When you or your little one is feeling a bit off, just add water. Sometimes all it takes is a few drinks of water, splashing in a puddle, or a relaxing bath to turn the day around." **Bre Grzych**

"I had three sons in 34 months...life was like a rollercoaster. We had our ups and downs. But life would not be the same without them." **Clara Murphy**

"Be kind to yourself. No need to 'jump back to normal.' Enjoy baby snuggles. Sleep when you can. Hydrate. Let friends bless you with meals or chores. Nursing requires you and your baby to learn from each other. It's not always easy, but so worth it." **Noelle Epp**

"Remind your baby daily, 'You are loved the whole outside full'." **Eva Mintz**

"I promise that you'll sleep again. I know it might feel like you'll never sleep more than 2 -4 hours at a time ever again, but you will and it will feel glorious." **Ashley Ludlow**

"No baby is exactly alike. No one knows a baby like its momma. There will be hurdles but trust your intuition. Allow yourself to be guided by your inner wisdom and the deep bond you share. You were made to do this!" **Lindsay Bednar**

"How are you feeling? Amazed? Sore? Tired? Overwhelmed? Proud? Perhaps you're struggling with the 'easiest most natural thing in the world,' feeding your newborn babe. This saying is ridiculous. Nursing for some is tough, although not impossible. It's your life and your baby.

Remember you are not alone." **Pat McBride**

"As a new Mama, allow yourself to be helped abundantly. When someone offers you support, accept it. When you feel overwhelmed, say: 'Would you be willing to help me with ___.'
Get your needs met, Mama." **Fabienne Fredrickson**

"Each breastfeeding journey is uniquely yours. Warmly embrace your unique situation and remember you CAN do hard things." **Rachel Poulsen**

"You've got this! Moms share the same fear: 'Am I equipped to take care of this baby?' Yes and it will be the greatest & most beautiful accomplishment. Sending you love! Reach out to others when you need help." **Camden Brown**

"After a long day of motherly duties, I felt special to receive a tap of encouragement from my baby boy while nursing." **Crystal Toller**

"It's extremely important to start early. I've been working with kids for more than 25 years.
If you have a concern, get it addressed right away to help guide good growth!" **Marisa Santos**

"Build your village - identify those special people that nourish and support you so that you can nourish and support your baby. They will help and are just waiting to be asked." **Tammy Button**

"The best you can do is to learn to live in the moment. There will be millions of precious events, big and small, through your journey of motherhood. If experienced in a hurry, all will pass in a blink of an eye." **Ira Baykovska**

"Dear Momma, the journey may be hard but the destination is worth every worry, frustration, sleepless nights, and shower-less days. Keep pushing forward and don't give up!" **Margaret Stoch**

"Love grows in quiet moments, whispered endearments, tender embraces, and while providing food/ nourishment for life. Nursing can be all of those.
Your desire to nurse deserves the support it needs." **Karen Kroczek**

About the Author

Dr. Catherine (Cathy) Murphy is a mom of two on a mission to transform health care from short term solutions to life enhancing treatments. From an early age, holistic options intrigued Cathy. She still has the first book she purchased about alternative therapies which included face massage, essential oils, craniosacral therapy and more. It wasn't until the birth of her son in the stormy summer of 2016 that she made the commitment to open her heart to holistic health.

Dr. Murphy is an orthodontist in a cozy Indiana suburb of Chicago, IL. Viewing the mouth as the mirror of one's overall health is the fuel to her passion for dentistry and health care.

Visit Catherine's website @ **www.drcatherinemurphy.com** and

In Harmony Orthodontics @ **www.inharmonyorthodontics.com**

About the Illustrator

Ira Baykovska is a children's book illustrator and a mom of two beautiful girls. Creating the illustrations for this book has been an amazing experience for her as she understands the struggles that come with nursing.

Ira has been drawing for as long as she can remember and sometimes cannot believe that this hobby has become her life-long career.

She has been working as freelance illustrator since 2014 and has illustrated more than 20 books for kids. Ira has a degree in Graphic Design and currently lives and works in Lviv, Ukraine.

Visit Ira's website **www.baykovska.com**

www.ingramcontent.com/pod-product-compliance
Lightning Source LLC
Chambersburg PA
CBHW041615120626
46551CB00002B/448